Happy Easter to:

Busy, Busy Bunnies

Coloring Book

Mary Lou Brown & Sandy Mahony

HAPPY
EASTER

Happy Easter!

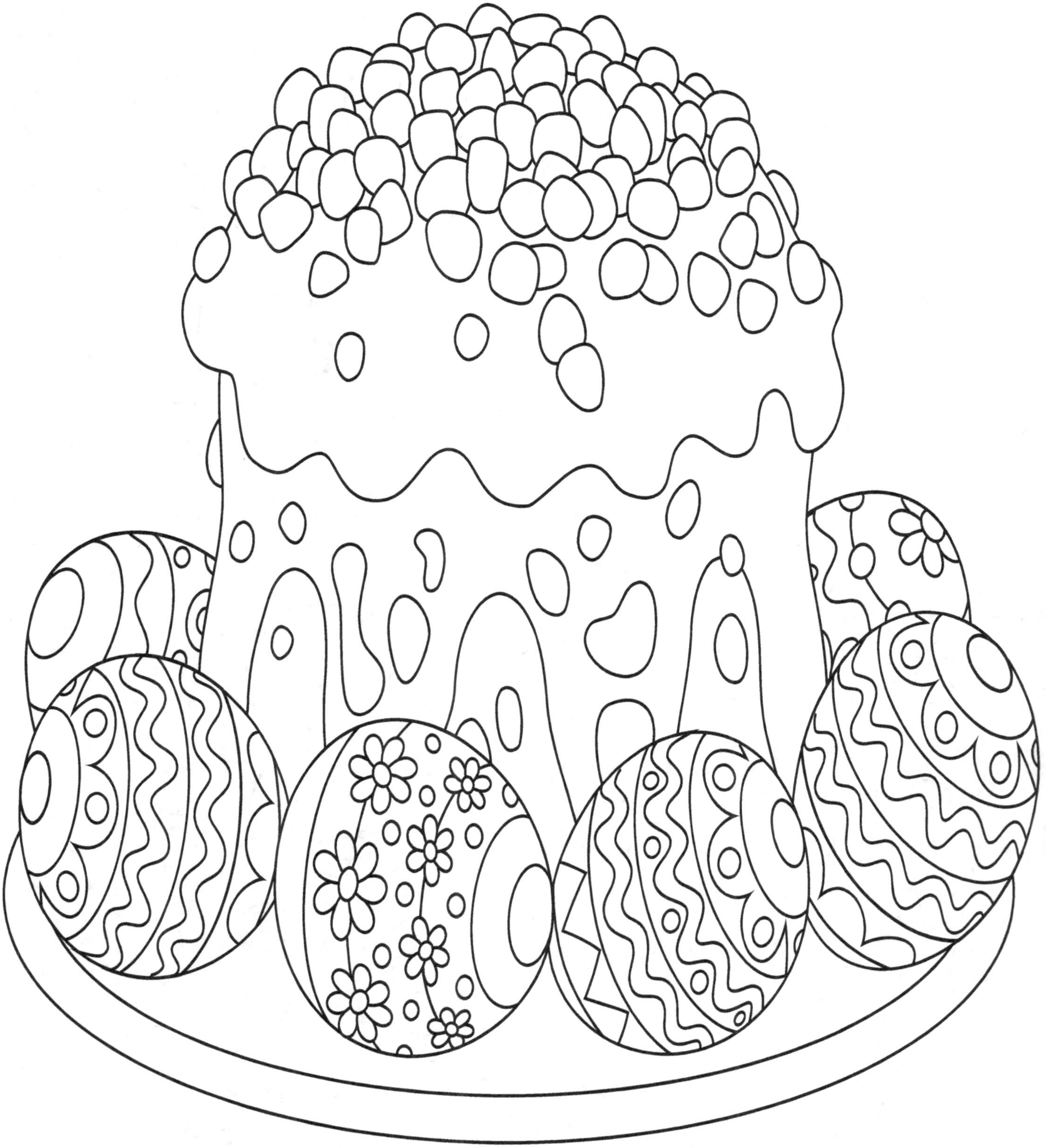

adventurelearningpress.com

www.ingramcontent.com/pod-product-compliance
Lightning Source LLC
Chambersburg PA
CBHW081536280526
45788CB00010B/3260
9781523800148